DOMINICAN REPUBLIC

by Jeri Cipriano

Red Chair Press   Egremont, Massachusetts

Look! Books are produced and published by Red Chair Press:

Red Chair Press LLC   PO Box 333   South Egremont, MA 01258-0333

www.redchairpress.com

Publisher's Cataloging-In-Publication Data

Names: Cipriano, Jeri S.

Title: Dominican Republic / by Jeri Cipriano.

Description: Egremont, Massachusetts : Red Chair Press, [2019] | Series: Look! books : Hello neighbor | Interest age level: 004-008. | Includes index, Now You Know fact boxes, a glossary and resources for further reading. | Summary: "Like any neighbor, the United States and the Dominican Republic share many things that are alike and many things that are different. In this book, readers discover how much children in the U.S. have in common with children in the Dominican Republic."--Provided by publisher.

Identifiers: ISBN 9781634403306 (library hardcover) | ISBN 9781634403726 (paperback) | ISBN 9781634403351 (ebook)

Subjects: LCSH: Dominican Republic--Social life and customs--Juvenile literature. | Dominican Republic--Description and travel--Juvenile literature. | United States--Social life and customs--Juvenile literature. | United States--Description and travel--Juvenile literature. | CYAC: Dominican Republic--Social life and customs. | Dominican Republic--Description and travel. | United States--Social life and customs. | United States--Description and travel.

Classification: LCC F1934.2 .C56 2019 (print) | LCC F1934.2 (ebook) | DDC 972.93 [E]--dc23

LCCN: 2017963470

Photo credits: iStock except for the following; p. 8, 9, 22: Dreamstime; Cover: RosaIreneBetancourt/Alamy; p. 7: Jeff Greenberg/Alamy; p. 17: Lucas Vallecillos/Alamy; p. 18: AAA Photostock/Alamy; p. 19: Reinhard Dirscherl/Alamy

Printed in the United States of America

0918 1P CGS19

Table of Contents

All About Dominican Republic

Hola! (OH-la) from the Dominican Republic. *Hola* is Spanish for "hello."

Dominican Republic is a country in the Caribbean (kuh-RIB-ee-uhn) Sea. It shares an **island** with Haiti. The island shared by these two neighbors is called Hispaniola.

FLORIDA U.S.A.

4

Atlantic
Ocean

CUBA

HAITI

DOMINICAN
REPUBLIC

PORT-AU-PRINCE

★ Santo
Domingo

JAMAICA

Carribbean Sea

Dominican Republic was the first stop **Christopher Columbus** made in 1492. It is one of the oldest countries of the Americas.

The flag of Dominican Republic is red, white and blue. The Dominican **coat of arms** is in the center.

Good to Know

When someone says the *Americas*, they mean North America, Central and South America. That's a big neighborhood!

Dominican money is the Dominican *peso* [PAY-so]. Paper bills show important people and places.

The **national** sport is baseball. Some of the world's best players are Dominicans.

Good to Know

U.S. money is the only money that is just one color—green. What people and places do you see on U.S. bills?

8

"Big Papi" David Ortiz is one of the best Dominican players ever. Can you name others?

The **capital** of the Dominican Republic is Santo Domingo. It is a very old city. There are buildings built in the 1500s, about 500 years ago.

Good to Know

The capital of the United States is Washington, D. C. It was first planned in 1790.

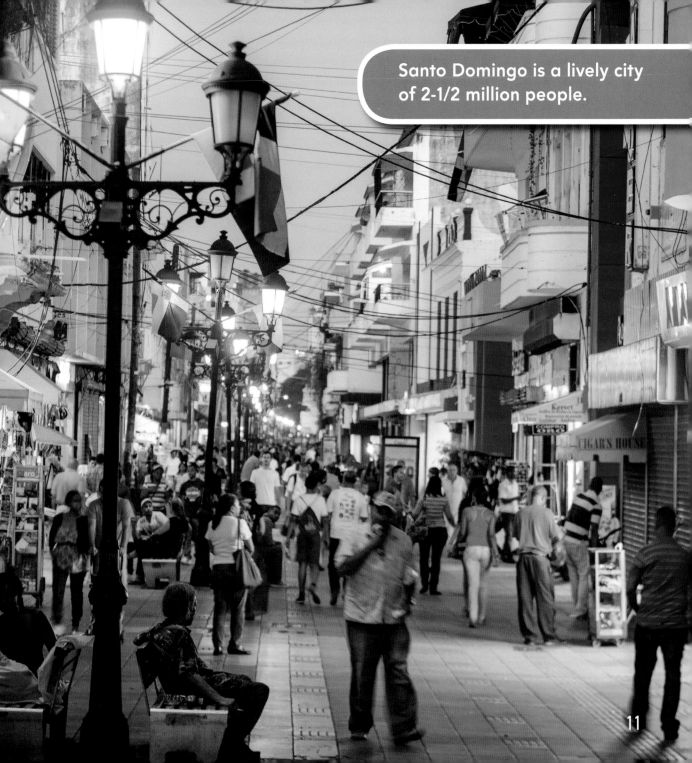

Santo Domingo is a lively city of 2-1/2 million people.

The Land

The Dominican Republic has a tropical climate. That means it is hot all year long. There are miles and miles of beautiful beaches.

Animals

Coral Reefs

They look like colorful rocks, but coral reefs are alive. They are made from many, many animals. Some are the size of pin heads.

Manatees

Manatees are called "sea cows." They are gentle animals that live in the water. They have "legs" that look like paddles.

14

Coral reefs look like colorful rock, but they are living animals.

The People

Dominicans are a mix of cultures: African, Spanish, French, and native Taíno.

Good to Know

People wear special clothes to dance to folk music.

Dominican music has an "Afro-Caribbean" sound.

First People

Taíno people lived in the Dominican Republic for thousands of years before Christopher Columbus arrived in 1492.

Taíno people grew corn, sweet potatoes, and other crops. Each village had a man or woman chief, or leader.

You can still find Taíno carvings in rock walls and caves.

Good to Know

The Taíno people carved large canoes out of wood. There was room to seat up to 150 people.

Celebrations

In February, <u>Carnival</u> celebrates all the different people who make their home in Dominican Republic.

Independence Days

Yes, there are two days. On February 27, Dominicans celebrate **independence** from Haiti in 1844. On August 16, Dominicans celebrate independence from Spain.

Words to Keep

capital: city that is home to the government

Christopher Columbus: first European believed to sail to North America in 1492

coat of arms: the special sign of a nation in the shape of a shield

independence: being free from control of others

island: a piece of land with water all around it

national: having to do with a country or nation

Learn More at the Library

Books (Check out these books to learn more.)

Rogers, Lura and Barbara Radcliffe. *Dominican Republic: Enchantment of the World*, 2nd edition. Children's Press, 2008.

Spengler, Kremena T. *The Dominican Republic: A Question and Answer Book*. Capstone Press, 2005.

Index

About the Author

Jeri Cipriano has written and
edited many books for young readers.
She likes making new friends
from different places. Jeri
lives and writes in New York state.